Short Walks in Auckland

Dog Friendly Walks

Part Three

By Helen Wenley and Grace Haden

Map source: openstreetmap.org

Auckland Public Transport Buses and Trains information: www.maxx.co.nz

ABOUT AUCKLAND

New Zealand consists of two main islands with unimaginative names - the North Island and the South Island.

Auckland sits on an isthmus in the North Island between two harbours - Waitemata Harbour to the north and Manukau Harbour to the south.

The population of Auckland is higher than any other New Zealand City - just over 1.4 million currently. It's still a small city on a global basis.

There have been many tourists who have thought that New Zealand was connected to Australia by a bridge and yet others like a relative of mine who admired the view from the Sky Tower over lunch and confused the Waitemata Harbour with Cook Strait (the waters between the North and South Island).

Auckland is a city with lots of green spaces and native bush. There are many walks within Auckland away from the hustle and bustle of city life. There are some areas that are so close to residential houses or city streets and yet, you could feel very isolated because of the surrounding native bush.

Short Walks in Auckland aims to get you closer to Auckland, to learn about the history, the people, the geography, the geology, the flora and fauna, historic places and many other surprises which even well seasoned locals will be surprised to find.

We wish to encourage you to get out and about; to discover Auckland on foot, so that you can feel a real sense of belonging, appreciation and excitement about what this unique and diverse city has to offer.

Getting Started...

Keep your dog/s in sight and under effective control in off leash areas.

Dog droppings must be removed.

Dogs are not permitted on sport fields or near children's playgrounds.

Wear comfortable shoes to avoid sore feet (in winter prepare for mud and puddles).

Take water to sip, especially on hot summer days, for you and your dog.

Use sunscreen even on cloudy days.

Build up slowly if it's been a while since you exercised (take rest stops – most times you will find a park bench, and remember it's not a race!)

Walk with a 4 legged and/or human companion.

Walks with Dogs

Auckland Council has designated dog friendly off leash exercise areas throughout Auckland. To help you discover these areas for your dog, we have included many of them in our circular walks (check the current regulations at the Auckland Council website - see the Resources section at the end of this book).

The walks do include areas where your dog is required to be on leash, under control and used to road traffic. As a dog owner you will be familiar with the on and off leash signs used by the Council.

We have provided a list of dog friendly beaches in the "Resources" section.

Each walk provides a different aspect of Auckland's urban landscape, to help you and your furry companion discover new mini adventures.

As with all our circular walks, start and end points can be varied.

Note: Not all of these walks have an off leash dog exercise area, but have been chosen because they are enjoyable walks.

Helen Wenley and Grace Haden

CONTENTS

1. Parnell Markets & Reserves

Parnell is Auckland's charming, historic shopping village. It was established in 1841 and is Auckland's first suburb. Parnell is a tourist mecca and a thriving centre for creative businesses. The shops are unique and there are abundant cafes and restaurants. Parnell has access to various parks and reserves—the Auckland Domain, the Parnell Rose Garden, Scarborough Reserve and Alberon Reserve. Source: *www.parnell.net.nz*

We walk from the busy bustling markets to the peacefulness of reserves with birdlife, nikau palms and New Zealand native ferns, past quaint cottages and the massive Holy Trinity Cathedral and the more modest St John the Baptist Church.

This is a great walk if you wish to take in both markets on a Saturday or you can exclude them if you prefer a quieter walk. Dog friendly with off-leash exercise areas.

Parnell Village is a popular shopping strip with many cafes and restaurants to choose from. To make this a full day outing, you may wish to stay and explore Parnell Village and learn about its history. Visit *www.parnell.net.nz – visiting Parnell* for information.

Nearby Attractions:

Parnell Holy Trinity Cathedral, Parnell Rose Garden,
Auckland Museum

Description: A mix of level paths and steep paths/steps. **Caution:** Muddy and slippery when wet. Suitable for most ages and levels of fitness and mobility, designed with flat shoes or running shoes in mind. Not suitable for wheelchairs and pushchairs.

To see: NZ native ferns palms and cycads, Waitemata Harbour views, farmers markets, old cottages.

Time: approx. 45 minutes. (about 3.92kms)

Cafés: la Cigale, 69 St Georges Bay Road, Rosehip Café, 82 Gladstone Road

Public toilets: In Parnell Road north of Denby Street

Children's playgrounds: None

Dogs: Off leash exercise areas

Picnic Site: Pick your favourite spot for your picnic rug. There are large picnic tables in Scarborough Reserve.

Directions:

Start from the Staffa Street (off Stratford Street) entrance.

1. Enter Alberon Reserve from Staffa Street.

2. Turn right > onto the boardwalk – nikau palms and ferns.

3. Turn right > at next junction.

4. Turn right > at concrete steps.

5. Turn left < after the steps then keep following the path and keep to the right.

6. Follow the concrete path thru reserve and turn right > at the junction (dog off-leash exercise area).

7. At the end of the reserve, turn left < into St Georges Bay Road

8. Come out of St Georges Bay Rd, turn left < then cross over Parnell Road at the lights and turn left < along Parnell Road.

9. Cross over Burwood Crescent and Claybrook Road, contunue straight ahead.

10. Turn right > into Domain Drive.

11. Turn left < into Titoke Street to visit Farmers Market (open Saturdays 8am to 12 noon).

12. Retrace steps to Domain Drive, cross the Drive and turn left <.

13. Turn right > into Forest Walk/Domain Walk.

14. Keep right > at the junction.

15. At the next junction follow the Domain Walk to Parnell down the steps to the   right >.

16. Turn right > at the next junction to Parnell via Railway Underpass and Ngahere Terrace.

17. Down at the railway track turn left < towards rail yards and then a quick right > to the Parnell Walk sign.

18. Go up the steps and at the top of the steps go straight ahead (centre fork) up the slight hill (Gibraltar Crescent).

19. Back onto Parnell Road, cross over at the pedestrian crossing on your left < and keep to the left–hand side of St John the Baptist

church into Denby Street.

20. At the end of Denby Street turn right > and then immediately left < down the brick paved lane into Scarborough Reserve (dog off leash exercise area and large picnic tables).

21. Turn left < at the exit of Scarborough Reserve.

22. Then right > into the carpark (La Cigale cafe). French Farmers markets are held here every Saturday and Sunday morning.

23. From the front Carpark - keep the building and shed on your left <.

24. At the end, keep following building around to the left <.

25. Turn left < at the wooden boardwalk into Alberon Reserve, go up steps.

26. Straight ahead the turn left < at the steps and proceed down the steps.

27. Turn right > at end of the path back into Stratford Street.

28. For the nearest café turn left < into Gladstone Road, to the Rosehip Café at #82.

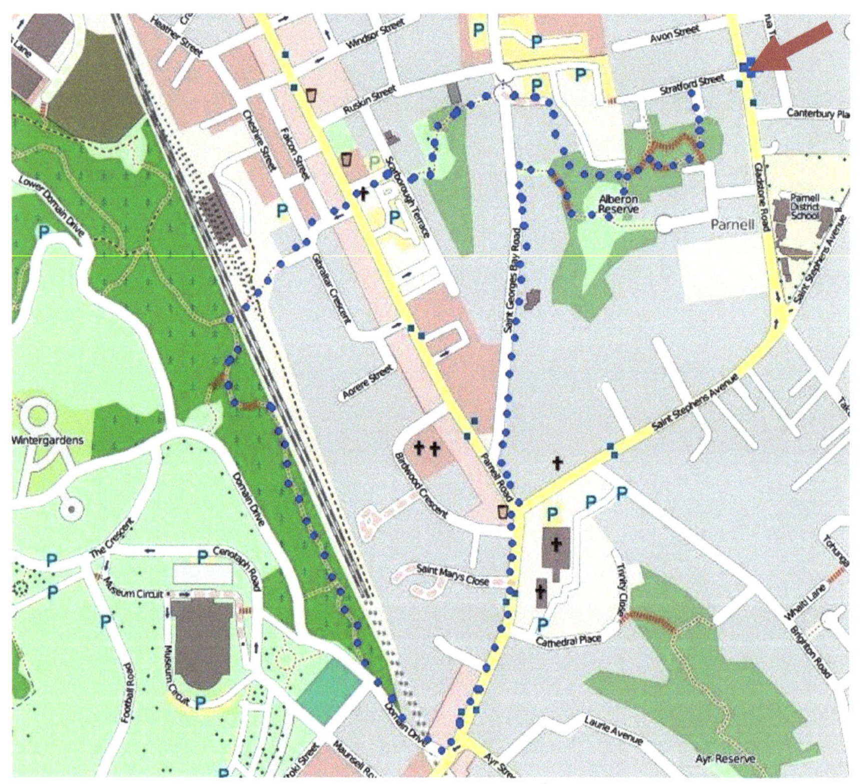
Heather Street
Windsor Street
Avon Street
Stratford Street
Canterbury Pla
Ruskin Street
Cheshire Street
Falcon Street
Scarborough Terrace
Alberon Reserve
Gladstone Road
Parnell District School
Lower Domain Drive
Saint Stephens Avenue
Parnell
Gibraltar Crescent
Saint Georges Bay Road
Aorere Street
Saint Stephens Avenue
Wintergardens
Domain Drive
Birdwood Crescent
Parnell Road
Torhunga
Whatti Lane
Brighton Road
The Crescent
Cenotaph Road
Museum Circuit
Saint Marys Close
Trinity Close
Football Road
Museum Circuit
Cathedral Place
Laurie Avenue
Ayr Reserve
Domain Drive
Toki Street
Maunsell Ro
Ayr Street

2. Parnell & Hobson Bay

This is a **low tide walk** that takes you around the edge of Hobson Bay, via the **Freda Kirkwood Walkway** and along the back streets of Parnell finishing at the Shore Road Cafe.
(check the tides *www.m.metservice.com/marine/tides/auckland*)

Dog lovers have two reserves that are off-leash dog exercise areas.

Nature lovers can enjoy the Native Bush in Ayr Reserve (look out for the cheeky fantails).

Parts of the **Hobson Bay Walkway** include a boardwalk which hopefully will one day be extended to make this walk accessible at high tide too.

Named after William Hobson – New Zealand's first governor – this bay is a tidal inlet. In the 1920s new transport routes were built to improve access to eastern Auckland with a train line going to Meadowbank.

Nearby walks:

Newmarket to Parnell, Parnell—markets and reserves, Parnell—Roses, trains and cranes, Remuera to Hobson Bay.

Description: A mix of level paths, steps and slightly inclined paths. Suitable for users of average fitness and mobility. May require boots in wet weather, running shoes suitable in dry weather.

NB Low-tide walk only

To see: Hobson Bay views, Rangitoto Island view, mangroves, native bush, fantails.

Time: approx. 60 minutes. (about 5 kms)

Cafés: Shore Road Café (cnr Seaview Road)

Public toilets: none nearby

Children's playgrounds: Thomas Bloodworth Park

Dogs: On and off leash

Picnic Sites: Seats only Ayr Reserve and Hobson Bay Walkway

Directions:

Start from Shore Road, Thomas Bloodworth Park, Car park.

1. Turn into the path that runs alongside the children's playground and the building (Terry   Jarvis Centre).

2. Follow the path around the Parnell Cricket building to the bridge and path that is signposted 'Hobson Bay Walkway, Shore Road Reserve'.

3. Take the next right > (after the bridge) along the boardwalk.

4. Cross the bridge to the right > and follow the path.

5. Head left < up the steps to Logan Terrace.

6. At the end of Logan Terrace, turn right > into Lichfield Road.

7. Turn right > into Waitoa Street.

8. Turn left < into Papahia Street.

9. Turn right > Awatea Road.

10. Turn right > into the walkway.

11. At the bottom of the steps, turn left < towards the water edge.

12. Turn right > at the water edge (explore to the left < if you wish).

13. At the top of the steps, turn left < keep to the inland path on the right >.

14. Turn right > at the Tohunga Crescent exit.

15. Turn right > into Whaiti Lane.

16. At the end of Whaiti Lane, turn right > into Brighton Road, cross Brighton Road and turn right >.

17. Turn left < into Kenderdine Lane and enter Ayr Reserve (off-leash dog exercise area).

18. Continue straight ahead (if you are lucky you might see fantail

birds along here).

19. Keep left < at the fork and cross the bridge over the stream.

20. Cross over Brighton Road to return to Shore Road.

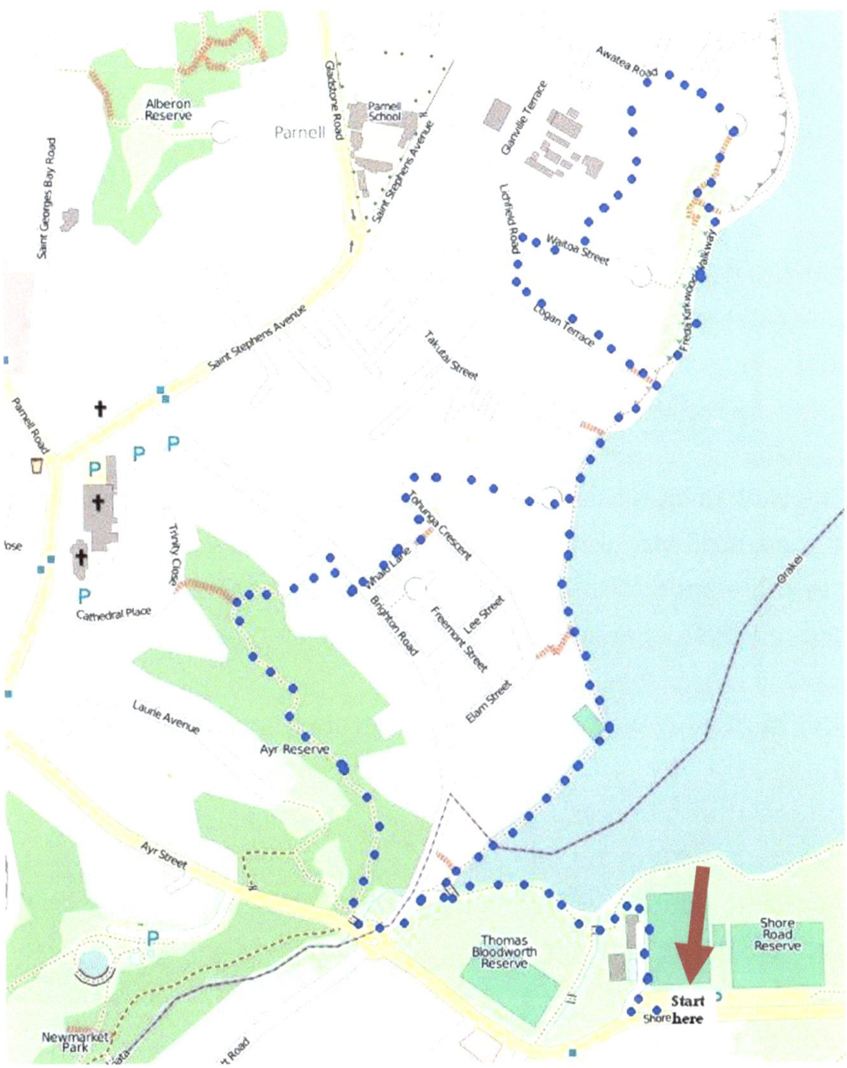

3. Onehunga Foreshore

The walk follows the edge of the Onehunga Bay Reserve and then the edge of Manukau Harbour. In summer, we would expect to see more shore birds. Even though the walk passes through part of the industrial area of Onehunga, it is still interesting.

This mostly flat walk can be accessed from Mangere Village also. There is a dog off-leash exercise area (gumboots required in winter/after rain), cycle paths and a children's playground.

Auckland Council is "currently restoring the foreshore next to Orpheus Drive to bring back a natural coastal edge and create recreational opportunities for the community. The project will provide high-quality open space, beaches, a boat ramp and picnic areas. A new bridge will connect the new land to the Onehunga lagoon." (source *www.aucklandcouncil.govt.nz*)

Onehunga was one of New Zealand's first and busiest ports. In the 1840's attractive Government legislation allowed settlers to buy land direct from Maori land owners on payment of a small tax to the government. Onehunga was seen as a key position in the military and naval defence of the western perimeter of Auckland and thus became one of the areas for Fencible settlement. (Fencibles were from the military pensioners and discharged soldiers in Great Britain. They would be known as 'The Royal New Zealand Fencibles' also referred to as Pensioners and were to become permanent settlers as well as a back-up military force.)

Nearby Attraction: TSB Bank Wallace Arts Centre, Pah Homestead. *www.onehunga.net.nz*

Description: A mainly flat walk with two bridges to cross. Suitable for users of average fitness and mobility. May require boots in wet weather, running shoes suitable in dry weather.

To see: Manukau Harbour shore and views, Mangere Mountain, Onehunga Wharf, Industrial area

Time: approx. 60 minutes. (about 5.77 kms)

Cafés: The Library Cafe and Columbus Coffee (plus selection of cafes and eateries in Onehunga Mall)

Public toilets: Onehunga Mall, Onehunga Bay Reserve

Children's playgrounds: Onehunga Bay Reserve

Dogs: Off leash area in Onehunga Bay Reserve (caution: muddy after rain so gumboots required)

Picnic site: Onehunga Bay Reserve

Directions:

Start from Onehunga Railway Station (Corner Princes Street and Onehunga Mall).

1. Cross over Onehunga Mall and continue straight ahead down Princes Street which then becomes Beachcroft Avenue.
2. Turn left < into Onehunga Bay Reserve and take the path past the playground heading towards the motorway side of the lagoon.
3. Turn left < to cross the motorway using the pedestrian bridge.
4. At the other side of the bridge, turn left < and follow Orpheus Drive along the edge of Manukau Harbour.
5. Continue following Onehunga Harbour Road past Onehunga Wharf.
6. At the bridge area, go up the ramp to the right and cross over to the boardwalk on the other side that continues along the harbour edge.
7. Follow the path until you reach Alfred Street. Turn left < into Alfred Street or continue a little further up to walk through Waikaraka Cemetery.
8. Turn left < into Neilson Street and then cross over to turn right > into Victoria Street.
9. Turn left < into Princes Street to return to the start.

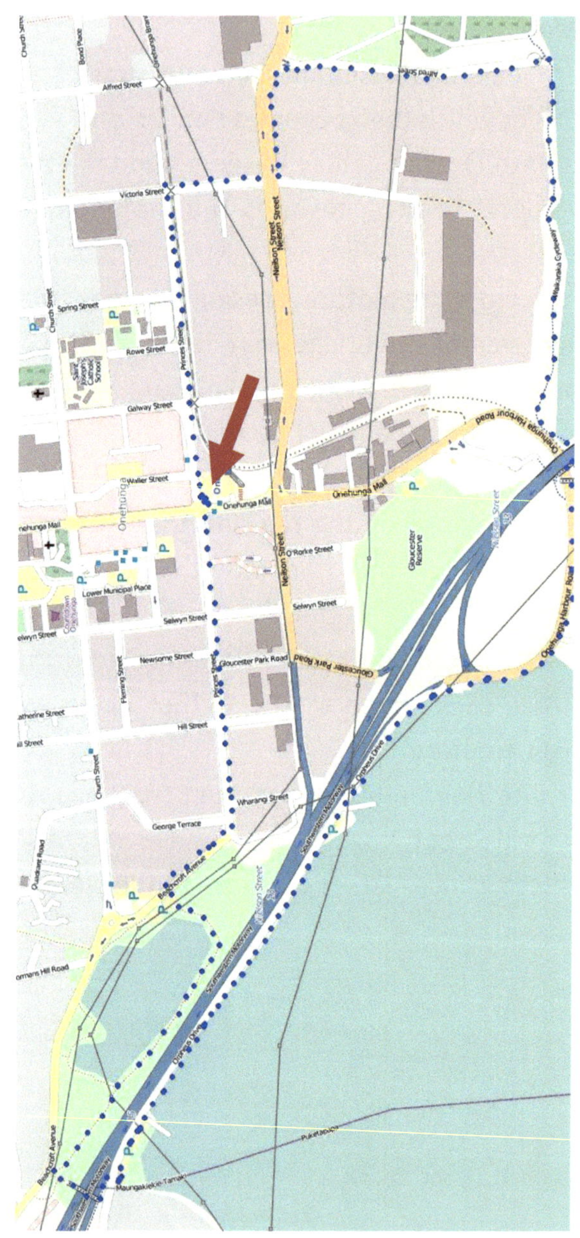

Church Street
Bond Place
Onehunga Bran
Alfred Street
Alfred Street
Waiapaka Crescent
Nelson Street
Nelson Street
Victoria Street
Spring Street
Church Street
Rowe Street
Princes Street
St Joseph Catholic School
Galway Street
Onehunga Harbour Road
Walter Street
Onehunga Mall
Onehunga Mall
Onehunga Mall
Onehunga Mall
Nelson Street
O'Rorke Street
Gloucester Reserve
Nelson Street
Lower Municipal Place
Selwyn Street
Selwyn Street
Onehunga Harbour Road
Selwyn Street
Newsome Street
Fleming Street
Gloucester Park Road
Gloucester Park Road
Pages Street
Catherine Street
Hill Street
Hill Street
Church Street
Wharang Street
England Drive
George Terrace
Onitaoru Road
Bycroft Avenue
Selwyn Street
Neilson Motorway
Southwestern Motorway
ormans Hill Road
Orange Drive
Puketapu
Bycroft Avenue
Southwestern Motorway
Maungakiekie-Tamaki

4. Herne Bay Parks and Reserves

Grey Lynn, Central Auckland

This walk explores both **Cox's Bay Reserve** and **Grey Lynn Park**. Cox's Bay Reserve is made up of three parks - Hukanui Reserve where the new boardwalk is, Bayfield Park where you may wish to have your picnic, and the sports fields of Cox's Bay Park. It is a mini-paradise for dog owners with off-leash dog exercise areas.

And it is family friendly too, with a selection of children's playgrounds and picnic sites. It is a great place for joggers and people who like to use the outdoor fitness stations.

The wide open spaces, sculptures, playing fields, the creek, mangrove swamps, gullies, the bay itself, a field with cattle and tall mature trees surrounded by interesting residential housing, make this another walk that is full of variety.

Grey Lynn is named for Sir George Grey (14 April 1812 – 19 September 1898), Governor of South Australia, twice Governor of New Zealand, Governor of Cape Colony (South Africa), Premier of New Zealand, and, towards the end of his life, Member Of Parliament for Auckland West.

Many of the houses were built between the 1880s and the beginning of the First World War. The houses provide interest along the route as very few of the originals have been completely replaced.

Nearby Walks: Western Springs and Meola Creek

Description: Paved walkways, steps, inclines and board walks. Suitable for users of average fitness and mobility.

To see: Sculptures, playing fields, the creek, mangrove swamps, gullies, the bay itself, a field with cattle and tall mature trees surrounded by interesting residential housing.

Time: approx. 70 minutes. (about 5.58 kms)

Cafés: Richmond Road shops

Public toilets: Grey Lynn Park

Children's playgrounds: Cox's Bay Reserve and Grey Lynn Park

Dogs: Off leash exercise areas—check signage for rules.

Picnic sites: Cox's Bay Reserve and Grey Lynn Park

Directions:

Start from Westmoreland Street West, Grey Lynn (off Richmond Road).

1. Cross Richmond Road, turn right > and turn left < to enter the Cox's Creek Walkway opposite Westmoreland Street West.
2. Continue straight ahead until you reach a cross path junction.
3. Turn left < and follow the path around the playing field of Cox's Bay Park, past the changing sheds and toilets.
4. Turn right > alongside West End Road with a view of Cox's Bay.
5. Follow the walkway straight ahead back around the other side of the playing fields.
6. At the cross path junction turn left < and cross the bridge into Bayfield Park.
7. Turn right > at the next junction and cross another bridge.
8. Continue straight ahead into Hukanui Crescent.
9. Continue straight ahead along Parawai Crescent.
10. Take the next left < into Tawariki Street (signposted to Moira Reserve).
11. At the very end of Tawariki Street, turn right > into the walkway beside #41.
12. Cross over Moira Street, continue straight ahead.
13. Turn left < into Richmond Road, then cross over at the pedestrian crossing, continue left <.
14. Turn right > into Farrar Street. Cross Jessel and Cockburn Streets.
15. Enter Grey Lynn Park at the very end of Farrar Street.
16. Continue straight ahead until you reach a 4 way junction and the entrance to "The Grey Lynn Sculpture Park".
17. Enter the gully "Sculptura", and continue straight ahead.
18. Take the left < path to Rose Road and follow the road around the corner to the right > into Arnold Street.
19. Re-enter Grey Lynn Park via the Arnold Street entrance.

20. Continue straight ahead at the junction and follow the path past the basketball hoops and public toilets.

21. Turn right > into Dryden Street.

22. Turn left < into Cockburn Street, cross the road, turn left <.

23. Turn right > into the Cox's Creek Walkway (between #58 & #33).

24. Take the left < fork, cross Sackville Street, turn left < along Sackville Street.

25. Turn right > into walkway between #27a and the pensioner flats.

26. Turn left < into Westmoreland Street West and follow the road to the right > to return to the start.

5. Westhaven & Point Erin

This loop walk utilises a new pathway Auckland Council has built which runs alongside the motorway, with panels that effectively screen the motorway traffic noise. It promises to be beautiful in December when the red flowers of the pohutukawa trees are in bloom.

Signs alongside the marina are announcing plans to make improvements too.

The route takes you alongside the marina on Westhaven Drive, crosses the motorway via the pedestrian bridge, follows the walkway along the motorway then up through the dog off leash exercise area in the reserve at Point Erin, then heads down along the harbour edge, under the Harbour Bridge.

Nearby Attractions: Harbour Bridge Climb, Victoria Park Markets, Erin Point Pools

Description: A mix of level paths, one lot of steep steps. Suitable for users of average fitness and mobility. Running shoes suitable.

To see: Auckland City views, Rangitoto Island views, harbour views, Harbour Bridge.

Time: approx. 45 minutes. (about 4.24 kms)

Cafés: Sitting Duck Cafe

Public toilets: Westhaven Drive, Point Erin Park

Children's playgrounds: Point Erin Park

Dogs: On leash. Dog off leash exercise area in Point Erin Park.

Picnic Sites: Tables in Point Erin Park, harbour side seats

Directions:

Start from Auckland Harbour Bridge end of Westhaven Drive, Saint Mary's Bay.

1. Head long Westhaven Drive alongside the marina towards the City.
2. At the pedestrian motorway overbridge, continue up the steps and cross the bridge.
3. On the other side, turn right > and follow the pathway alongside the motorway to the very end.
4. Turn left < up the steps.
5. Turn hard left < at the path crossroads to come out beside Point Erin pool area.
6. Keep the pool to your right > and follow the pathway straight ahead.
7. Exit the Park at Sarsfield Street and turn right >.
8. Cross over Curran Street and turn right > along Curran Street.
9. Continue walking along the harbour edge, go under the harbour bridge and turn right into Westhaven Drive to return to the start.

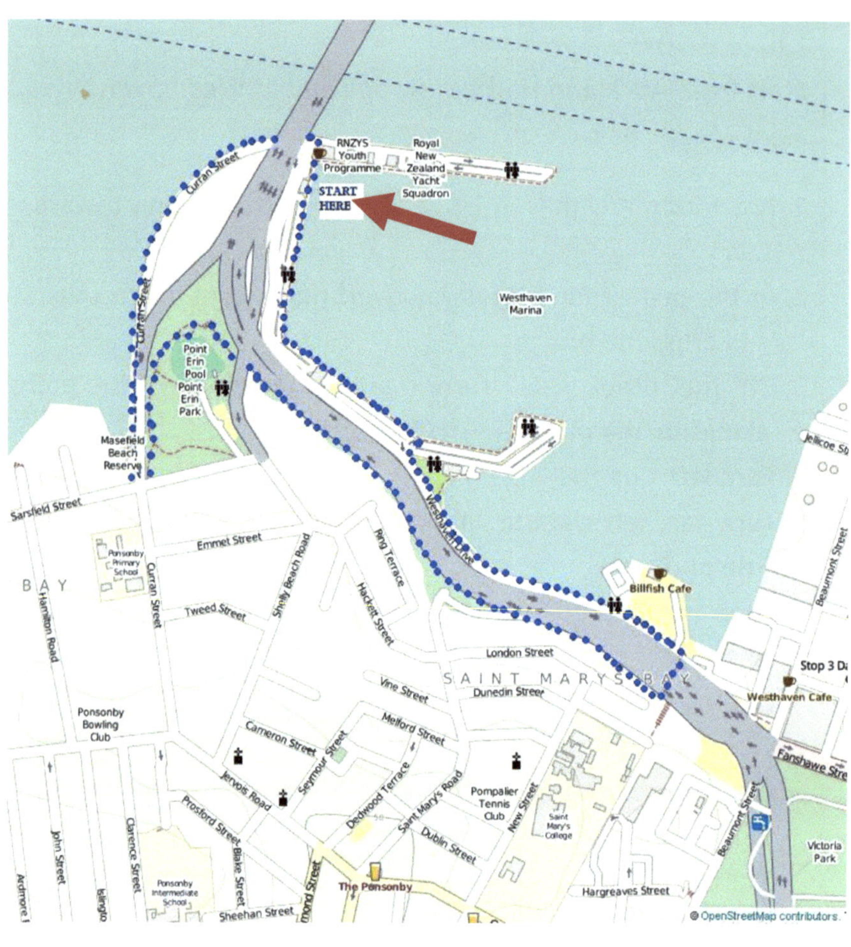

RNZYS Youth Programme
Royal New Zealand Yacht Squadron
START HERE
Westhaven Marina
Curran Street
Curran Street
Point Erin Pool
Point Erin Park
Masefield Beach Reserve
Sarsfield Street
Ponsonby Primary School
Emmet Street
Ring Terrace
Hamilton Road
Curran Street
Tweed Street
Shelly Beach Road
Hackett Street
Westhaven Drive
Billfish Cafe
Jellicoe St
Beaumont Street
BAY
Ponsonby Bowling Club
Cameron Street
Seymour Street
Melford Street
Vine Street
London Street
SAINT MARYS BAY
Dunedin Street
Stop 3 Da
Westhaven Cafe
John Street
Clarence Street
Islingto
Jervois Road
Prosford Street
Blake Street
Dedwood Terrace
Saint Mary's Road
Dublin Street
New Street
Pompalier Tennis Club
Saint Mary's College
Fanshawe Stre
Beaumont Street
Victoria Park
Ponsonby Intermediate School
Sheehan Street
mond Street
The Ponsonby
Hargreaves Street
Ardmore l
© OpenStreetMap contributors.

6. Unsworth Reserve

Over the years, we have made many visits to Paul Matthews Road off the Upper Harbour Highway in Albany totally unaware that nearby is the huge **Unsworth Reserve** with the **Alexandra Stream** flowing through.

In 2013 a new board walk/ cycle way was completed. Obviously we have no idea what was here previously, and can't imagine how much the project would have cost, but it certainly looks impressive. We hope that it will get a lot of use by recreational and commuting cyclists, pedestrians and joggers. As the many plants and trees grow, it will become a beautiful oasis in the middle of suburban housing.

Along the boardwalk are boards - informing us of ways that water quality is being improved, the past fruit cultivation, ways to reduce erosion and plants - the weeds and natives. And we are impressed with the sign posting.

It was fabulous to walk among many silver ferns, ponga ferns and manuka trees beside the untouched paths along the edge of the reserve – a bush track that is also an off leash dog exercise area.

As we were about to return to the industrial edge of the reserve, we were delighted to spot a pair of adult ducks with about 10 to 12 ducklings swimming and feeding among the reeds in the wetlands of the storm water catchment Omega Pond.

The Alexandra Stream is thought to be named after Princess Alexandra who married the Prince of Wales in 1863.

Description: Mostly level paths. Suitable for most ages and levels of fitness and mobility, designed with flat shoes or running shoes in mind. Suitable for wheelchairs and pushchairs.

To see: Wetlands, park land, ponds.

Time: approx. 60 minutes (about 5.0 kms).

Cafés: Café Drina, Paul Matthews Road.

Public toilets: Rosedale Park

Children's playgrounds: Unsworth Reserve

Dogs: Off leash areas: on Bush tracks

Picnic Sites: Take your own rugs and picnic gear.

Directions:

Start from Rosedale Park (off Jack Hinton Drive, Paul Matthews Road).

1. From the carpark, turn right > down Jack Hinton Drive.
2. Cross Paul Matthews Road and enter pathway opposite.
3. Continue straight ahead through the road tunnel and keeping to the main path.
4. Turn right > into Barbados Drive, cross over and enter the boardwalk leading into Unsworth Reserve.
5. Continue directly through the reserve.
6. Turn left < into Goldfinch Rise.
7. Turn left < into Caribbean Drive.
8. Turn left < back into Unsworth Drive take the right–hand path and keeping right >.
9. Turn left < into Mallard Place.
10. Cross over Barbados Drive.
11. Turn right > then left < into Rook Place.
12. Turn left < onto pathway between #12 & #7 Rook Place.
13. Rejoin the main pathway to go through tunnel.
14. Turn left < at the ponds.
15. Turn right > into Omega Street.
16. Turn right > into Paul Matthews Road.
17. Cross over Paul Matthews Road to enter Rosedale Park on the left < and return to the start.

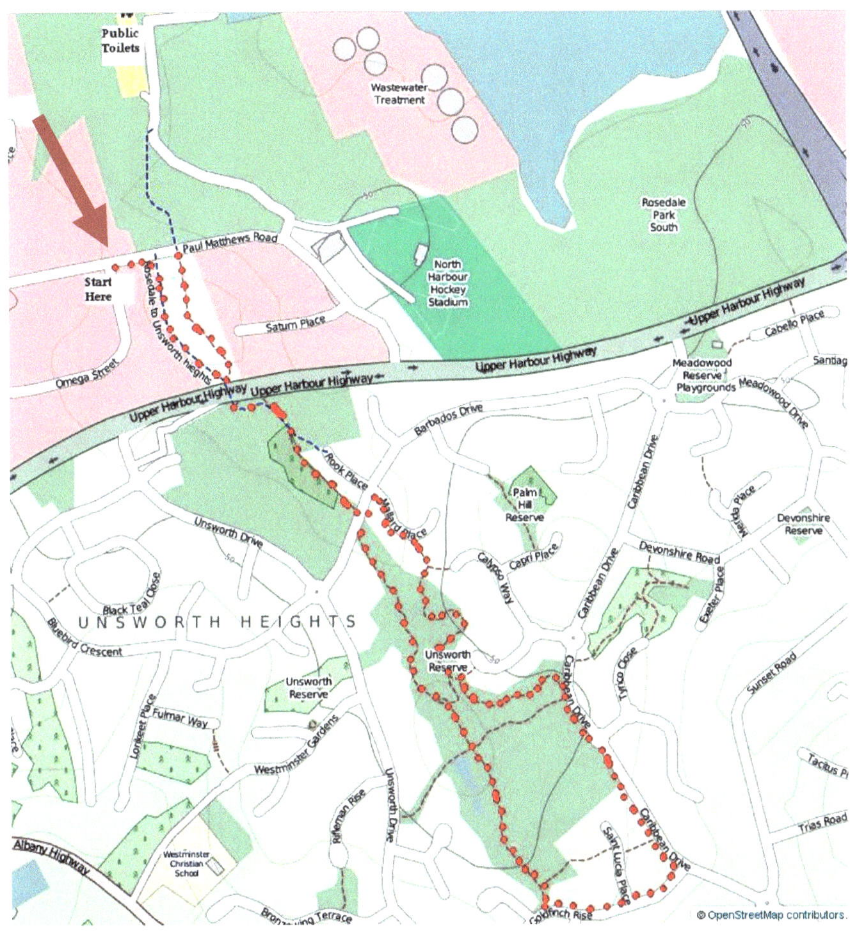

Public Toilets
Wastewater Treatment
Rosedale Park South
Paul Matthews Road
Start Here
Rosedale to Unsworth heights
North Harbour Hockey Stadium
Saturn Place
Upper Harbour Highway
Omega Street
Upper Harbour Highway
Upper Harbour Highway
Upper Harbour Highway
Cabello Place
Santiag
Meadowood Reserve Playgrounds
Meadowood Drive
Barbados Drive
Rook Place
Mallard Place
Palm Hill Reserve
Caribbean Drive
Murillo Place
Devonshire Road
Devonshire Reserve
Calypso Way
Capri Place
Unsworth Drive
Black Teal Close
UNSWORTH HEIGHTS
Bluebird Crescent
Caribbean Drive
Exeter Place
Lyrico Close
Sunset Road
Unsworth Reserve
Longest Place
Fulmar Way
Unsworth Reserve
Westminster Gardens
Caribbean Drive
Tacitus Pl
Trias Road
Albany Highway
Westminster Christian School
Rifleman Rise
Unsworth Drive
Saint Lucia Place
Caribbean Drive
Bron... Terrace
Goldfinch Rise
© OpenStreetMap contributors.

7. Bayview Giant Kauri

Glenfield, North Shore Auckland

The walk starts off in **Lynn Reserve**, and heads up a bush filled gully with a small stream, to a **giant Kauri tree** (over 2 metres in diameter and is said to be about 800 years old) among a grove of smaller kauri trees which are growing in **Leigh Scenic Reserve**. It is awesome!

The route joins up with the **Glenfield Coastal Walkway** and heads around to the boat ramp and **Manuka Reserve** at the bottom of Manuka Road. Hearing the song of the tui birds as we slowly walked up the incline of Manuka Road gave us great encouragement.

This walk through the bush and along the Upper Harbour coastline is not only beautiful, it provides a great workout if you are into fitness. It is also a fun family walk that includes two children's playgrounds, plus off leash dog exercise areas.

The new playground at **Lynn Reserve** looks great, and there is also a new children's '**learn to cycle track**'.

The Glenfield area was once a large fertile area beside Hellyers Creek. It provided Maori settlers with plenty of food from the land and sea. Then the Europeans arrived, and converted the area from forestry to farming. It has now become an Auckland suburb. More information is available from Glenfield Library and the Glenfield Historical Society.

Nearby Walks: Northcote Point, Chelsea Bush, Bayview Bush and Coast.

Description: Bush track, steps, inclines and board walks. Muddy in places when wet. Suitable for users of average fitness and mobility.

To see: Native bush, including Giant Kauri, small waterfalls, views across Auckland Harbour to Hobsonville Point, native birds.

Time: approx. 75 minutes. (about 5.8 kms)

Cafés: None

Public toilets: Manuka Reserve, Lynn Reserve

Children's playgrounds: Lynn Reserve and Manuka Reserve, Spinella Reserve.

Dogs: Off leash areas.

Picnic sites: Lynn Reserve and Manuka Reserve.

Directions:

Start from Lynn Reserve, Bayview, near Glenfield.

1. Enter Lynn Reserve along right-hand side, go past playground and continue straight ahead to enter Leigh Scenic Reserve. Ignore very first path to the right.

2. Turn left < at the junction sign-posted to Morriggia Place. Go past the Giant Kauri.

3. Turn right > into Morriggia Place.

4. Turn left < into Bay View Road.

5. Turn right > into Cantina Avenue.

6. Turn right > into Bonito Place.

7. Turn left < track through Bonito Scenic Reserve and Spinella Reserve.

8. Cross over Spinella Drive and turn left < along Spinella Drive.

9. Turn right > along track in between #6 and #8 Spinella Drive that leads to Glastron Place.

10. Turn right > into Bay View Road.

11. Turn left < into Glendhu Road.

12. Enter the Glenfield Coastal Walkway and follow the track alongside the inlet (exit left < at Lynn Reserve for a shorter walk).

13. Note: There is a slightly tricky bit where a bridge crosses the stream – follow the path to the right > after crossing the bridge.

14. At the wide open green field follow the direction of the arrow on the post, heading for the far left-hand corner to pick up the walkway to Manuka Reserve (which has a lookout, picnic site, toilets and playground).

15. Turn left < into Manuka Reserve.

16. Cross over Lynn Road and turn left <.

17. Turn right > after #21 into Lynn Reserve.

18. Follow the track through the gully, up the steps to turn left <
alongside the end of Anne Maclean Drive, stay on the path.

19. Turn left < at the T-junction, rejoin the main path and return
to the start.

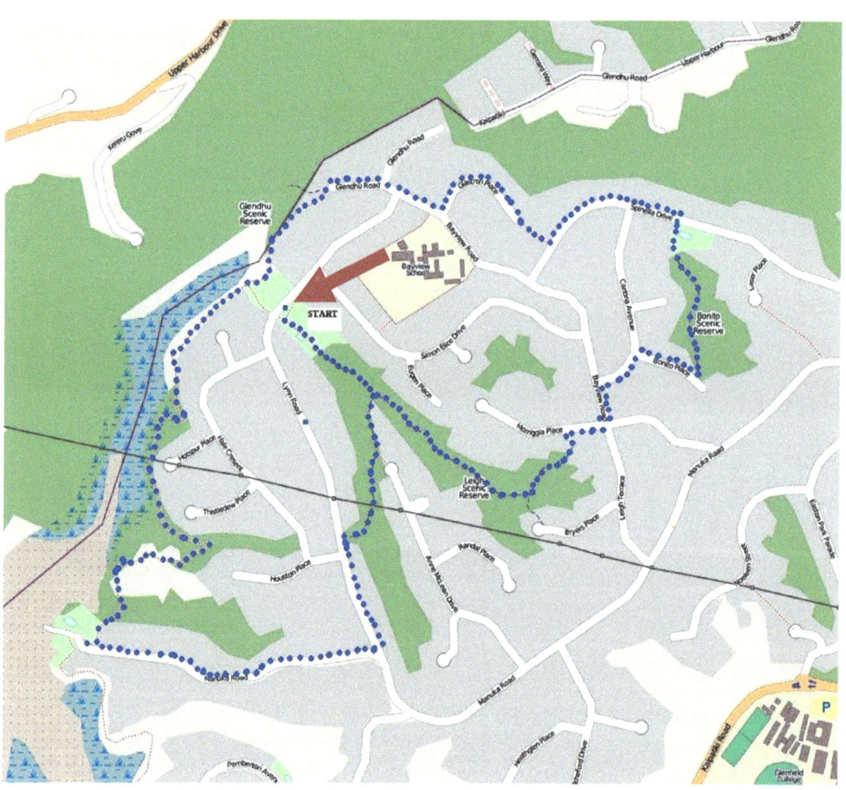

8. Otara Creek

Otara, South Auckland

The **Otara Creek Walkway** in South Auckland, passes through some 220 hectares of waterway/tidal mudflats and forms a green corridor within Otara township.

This huge reserve was almost empty of people when we visited; we saw two cyclists and one stray dog.

This walkway is ideal for **family cycling** and for taking your dog for an **off-leash walk**. (Dogs are welcome along the walkway provided they are kept under control and do not disturb wildlife or other park users. Dogs are not permitted on sport fields or near children's playgrounds.)

The creek has mangrove mud flats and is sadly polluted - the locals seems to take delight in dropping shopping trolleys into the creek. However, if you can overlook the neglect, you may find enjoyment in the bigger view: the sounds of the birds and the trees and the native plants within the **Otara Creek Reserve**.

Description: Mainly level paths,. Suitable for users of average fitness and mobility.

To see: Otara Creek and estuary

Time: approx. 75 minutes. (about 5.75 kms)

Cafés: None

Public toilets: Fair Mall Car Park

Children's playgrounds: Near the sports clubs

Dogs: Off leash in the reserve. Dogs are welcome along the walkway provided they are kept under control and do not disturb wildlife or other park users. Dogs are not permitted on sport fields or near children's playgrounds.

Picnic Sites: Seats only in Otara Creek Reserve

Directions:

Start from the car park in Fair Mall of Bairds Road, East Tamaki.

1. Cross over Bairds Road at the pedestrian crossing, turn right > along Bairds Road, then left < into Hayman Street.
2. Turn left < into Lovegrove Crescent.
3. Turn left < into Otara Creek Reserve.
4. Turn left < at the next junction.
5. Keep following the pathway alongside the creek.
6. At the sports field, take the higher concrete pathway.
7. Cross over Otara Road, and keep following the track beside the creek.
8. Exit into Gaye Crescent and turn right >.
9. Turn right > into Gilbert Road.
10. Turn left < into Franich Street.
11. Turn right > into Otara Road.
12. Turn right > into Bairds Road and return to the start.

Start here
Manukau Institute of Technology
Manukau Institute of Technology
Sir Edmund Hillary Collegiate
Otara Creek Reserve
Bairds Primary School
Mayfield School
East Tamaki Road
East Tamaki Road
East Tamaki Road
East Tamaki Road
East Tamaki Road
Otara
Highbrook Drive
Highbrook Drive
Highbrook Drive
Otara Road
Alexander Crescent
Alexander Crescent
Parker Crescent
Franklyn Road
Clyde Road
Gilbert Road
Bland Place
Lappington Road
Bairds Road
Bairds Road
Edward Avenue
Loxio Way
Lorien Place
Kerwyn Avenue
Arwen Place
Antrim Crescent
Tyrone Street
Johnstones Road
Williams Crescent
Harrelll Road
Darby Road
Vickter Crescent
Hills Road
Carey Place
Sean Fitzpatrick Place
Harwood Avenue
Ashton Avenue

9. Cascade Walkway

Howick, East Auckland

We would have been totally lost here without our maps (and even so, the maps do not show all footpaths). This area is an example of a wonderful resource that is not made easy for people to enjoy. We did ask a few dog walkers for directions, but they could not tell us where other paths went.

The paths are great for cycling and walking (with your dog and/or your children). There is diverse birdlife and native plants and trees. We were surprised by the lack of picnic/BBQ facilities, public toilets and children's playgrounds within the Cascade Reserve. However, we did come across 3 children's playgrounds in total, making this a family friendly walk. There are off leash dog exercise areas – look out for the signs.

Near the Historical Village is an area to play with marbles, and another area for kids to ride their bicycles on a specially made track.

Botany Creek forms a cascade waterfall which can be seen from a viewing platform. Native vegetation has been planted by local school children. Keep an eye out for monarch butterflies on a warm day.

The Cascade Farm was owned by Captain Robert Hattaway in the 1860's. Coaches used to travel to the farm near the Hattaway Bridge and you can still see the scoria paving stones. The macrocarpa trees by the bridge were planted by Maria Hattaway. Other large trees are a legacy of the Hattaway's settlement.

Nearby Attraction: The Cascade Walkway runs next to the Howick Historical Village, where you can experience life in Howick back in the 1800s. *www.fencible.org.nz*

Description: Mainly level paths and a few slightly inclined paths. Suitable for users of average fitness and mobility. Mostly concrete paths with a small stretch of dirt track under trees.

To see: Creeks, birdlife, small waterfall, bridges. View of Rangitoto Island, Pigeon Mountain, Mt Wellington, Waitakere Ranges and One Tree Hill

Time: approx. 75 minutes. (about 6 kms)

Cafés: The Homestead Cafe

Public toilets: Bell Park

Children's playgrounds: Gosford Drive, Highland Park Drive, Bell Park with Mountain Bike Trail & Marbles Game area

Dogs: On and off leash areas.

Picnic Sites: Seats and tables in Bell Park

Directions:

Start from Bells Road (off Cascades Road/Pakuranga Road).

1. Take the path at the left hand side of the Howick Historical Village (beside the Homestead Café).

2. Continue straight ahead alongside the fence down the hill.

3. Cross the bridge and turn right > and continue straight ahead.

4. Cross the Hattaway Bridge (after the Cascade viewing platform), turn left < and join the concrete path and keep going to the left <.

5. Keep to the main path alongside the creek.

6. At Botany Road, turn left < to cross the road bridge that goes over the creek.

7. On the other side, turn left < and follow the path alongside the creek again.

8. Cross the next bridge and take the next path to the right >.

9. Take the right fork > beside the Gosford Drive children's playground.

10. Exit to the left < at Levington Drive, continue straight ahead.

11. At the T-junction turn right > into Bradbury Road.

12. Cross over Bradbury Road, then turn left < into Highland Park Drive (Views of Rangitoto Island and Pigeon Mountain. Spot the Sky Tower, Mount Wellington, One Tree Hill and the Waitakere Ranges).

14. Keep going straight ahead at the roundabout.

15. Cross Aviemore Drive, turn left < then immediately right > into a service lane (beside the Mandarin Palace).

16. Turn left < onto the concrete walkway.

17. Cross the next bridge on your right > and continue up the path towards the pond.

18. Turn left < down the pohutukawa walkway.

19. At the roundabout take second exit to the left < and return to the start.

Waikaranga School
Highland Park
Howick Primary School
Juliet Avenue
Angel
Willoughby Avenue
The Link
Pakuranga Road
Howick Intermediate
Botany Road
Fortunes Road
Pigeon Mountain Road
Lilac Place
Buckland
Avenmore Drive
Tomkia Place
Atherleley Avenue
Ballater Place
Cromedale Avenue
Highland Park Drive
Hedge Row
Fortunes Road
Park Avenue
Centre Court
Village Drive
Bells Road
Sir Lloyd Drive
Dalwhinnie Parade
Bradbury Road
Union
Cascades Road
Tupaki Place
Harland Place
Bells Road
Start Here
Lady Marie Drive
Avenmore Drive
Lexington Drive
Victoria Court
Botany Road
Bombay
Kumai
Narvan Down Avenue
Walworth Avenue
Shortlap Street
Lewisham Street
Bradbury Road
Sandgate Avenue
Godfort Drive
P
Botany Downs
Hope Farm Avenue
Robson Alison Way
Reelick Avenue
Cascades Road
Pinewood Grove
Elim Christian College
Botany Road
Parramatta Place
Howick
Mirr
Ennis Av
Crescent
Headcom Place
Cascades Road
Northpark

10. Apriana St Johns

St Johns, East Auckland

This walk makes use of the reserves within walking distance of **Glen Innes Train Station**. We visit the horse paddocks of **Apirana Reserve** with views of Mount Wellington, Eastern Beach and on a clear day, the Coromandel (this is part of the 7.5km Point to Point Walkway) and then walk through the native bush within **St Johns Bush**.

St Johns Bush reserve is a green corridor for birds flying across Auckland. There is a wetland area with native fish. This area is home to over 165 different species of plants. The kauri tree is over 150 years old.

Keep your eyes and ears open to take in the native flora and fauna.

There is an off leash dog exercise area en-route.

Joining up reserves to minimize street walking is a challenge, but we are very fortunate to have so many green spaces in Auckland. Our dream is that sometime in the future, the reserves will be linked together to help us commute safely by bicycle or on foot (and hopefully wheelchairs), from one area to another, minimizing road use.

Description: A mix of level and slightly hilly paths. Suitable for users of average fitness and mobility.

To see: St Johns Bush native trees and ferns, residential housing, reserves, horse paddocks, views of Eastern Beach and the Coromandel, city skyline view

Time: approx. 60 minutes. (about 4.5 kms)

Cafés: Glen Innes, Columbus in Felton Matthew Avenue

Public toilets: Glen Innes

Children's playgrounds: Off John Shaw Drive (off Howard Felton Avenue) BMX Track—Merton Reserve

Dogs: On leash and off leash exercise area   Merton Reserve

Picnic Sites: Apirana Reserve

Directions:

Start from Glen Innes Train Station.

1. Turn left < along Apirana Avenue.

2. Turn left < into Apirana Reserve.

3. Follow the footpath straight ahead through the reserve, and then the track to the left < up the hill through the horse paddocks.

4. Turn left < into Saint Johns Road.

5. Turn right > into Gowing Drive.

6. Turn left < into Saint Johns Bush (between #131 and #133 Gowing Drive).

7. Follow track to the left < (signposted St Johns Road).

8. Cross St Johns Road at the pedestrian crossing and turn right > along St Johns Road.

9. At the roundabout, continue into College Road.

10. Turn left < into Strong Street.

11. Cross over Howard Hunter Avenue and turn right > along Howard Hunter Avenue.

12. Turn left < into Merton Reserve.

13. Follow the pathway straight ahead through Merton Reserve (past the BMX Track).

14. Cross over Felton Matthew Avenue to follow the pathway to return to Glen Innes Train Station.

Hawkins Street
Gowing Drive
Worcester Road
don Crescent
Saint Johns Bush
Saint Johns Road
Orakei
Saint John
Apirana Reserve
Apirana Avenue
Castledine Crescent
Melling Street
Eastview Road
Maungarahiri-Tamaki
Felton Mathew Avenue
Abraham Place
Sirken Avenue
Caulton Street
Norman Lesser Drive
Kissling Place
Waikato Place
gnaos Drive
Fridays Road
Thorp Street
Tisdall Crescent
Norman Lesser Drive
Cotton Street
Strong Street
Lush Avenue
John Shaw Drive
Swanston Road
Merton Road
Howard Hunter Avenue
Howard Hunter Avenue
BMX Track
Merton Reserve
Farmhouse Lane
Felton Mathew Avenue
Apirana Avenue
Northern Strategic North Island Main Trunk
Glen Innes

11. Hobsonville Point

Hobsonville, West Auckland

This family friendly walk explores the former air base with only a few of the old buildings remaining. There has been a great deal of development going on with new housing and the new ferry service to the CBD from 'The Landing' (which used to be the launching and landing place for flying boats, including Sunderland and Catalina planes). There is a rough track around the perimeter of Bomb Point where you can see munitions storage bunkers.

This walk takes about 60 minutes and is ideal for spring and autumn (too hot in summer and too muddy in winter). There is a lot to explore if you haven't been here before. This is a dog friendly walk with an off-leash area and is a mostly flat walk.

The former airbase was developed in 1925. It was a combined aerodrome making provision for both airplanes and seaplanes.

This site is now being developed for residential housing and the marine industry. The area is still undergoing change, and this walk may vary according to the current developments.
Get up-to-date information here:
www.hobsonvillepoint.co.nz/visit/parks-playtime

Nearby Attractions:

Weekend markets down by the Ferry Landing.
Fresh fruit and vegetables available at road stores along Hobsonville Road.
Catch the ferry to Hobsonville Point from the CBD for a day out (weekdays only at time of publication).

Description: Level sealed paths and bush track. Suitable for users of average fitness and mobility. May require boots in wet weather, running shoes suitable in dry weather. Suggested spring/autumn walk.

Caution: Muddy and slippery when wet.

To see: Hangars, barracks, officers housing, boatbuilding school, seaplane slipway, munitions storage bunkers, Auckland harbour views, weekend markets.

Time: approx. 60 minutes. (about 5.5 kms)

Cafés: Catalina Cafe

Public toilets: Catalina Café, The Landing

Children's playgrounds: Buckley Precinct

Dogs: Off and On leash areas

Picnic Sites: Seating in playground area

Directions:

Start from the Carpark (Buckley Avenue opposite Catalina Cafe).

1. Exit left < from the car park, and follow the path straight ahead along Buckley Avenue.

2. Turn right > into Marine Parade.

3. Turn left < into Marlborough Crescent (married officers housing).

4. Turn left < into Hudson Bay Road.

5. Turn left < down steps to head for the ferry terminal.

6. Continue along the water's edge to the right >.

7. Join Boundary Road and continue straight ahead.

8. Do the loop around Bomb Point.

9. At the end of Boundary Road, turn right > into Wallace Road (at time of publishing there is a temporary track signposted "Coastal Walkway" to use which is subject to change).

10. Turn left < into Onekiritea Road.

11. Turn left < at the end, then right > behind the bus shelter, onto track to the children's playground.

12. Cross Buckley Avenue into the wetlands opposite.

13. Follow the path alongside the wetland area, then continue along gravel track around field to return to the carpark.

Beach Road
Buckley Avenue
Auckland - Beach Haven
Cochrane Road
Sunderland Avenue
Neville Road
P
Hudson Bay Road
Ranburough Close
Bluff Parade
P
P
Hudson Bay Road
Start
Here
Hartridge Crescent
Binding Road
Hobsonville Point
Buckley Avenue
Leslie Street
Toheroa Street
De Havilland Road
Hobsonville Point Road
Onekiritea Road
Cropete Street
Hobsonville Point Primary School
Harvard Street
De Havilland Road
Meteor Road
Wallace Road
Walker Place
Culper Crescent
son Drive
Clark Road
Boundary Road

12. Henderson Creek

Henderson Creek, West Auckland

The previous Waitakere City Council has spent a great deal of ratepayers money on providing walkways and cycle-ways throughout the district. It was heartening to see people make the most of them as we walked alongside the Creek. When we visited there was work being carried out at the **"International Walkway of Trees"** .

We did enjoy our 5km walk - the sun was shining, the birds were singing, we were sheltered from the cool breeze and this was a part of Auckland that was new to us. To top it all off, we had a delicious coffee at The Falls Restaurant - sitting outside in the sunny courtyard.

Henderson Creek was once a hive of activity for traders, vintners, farmers, orchardists and families, and the area was also known for its timber milling industry.

There are off leash dog exercise areas within the reserves and parks – look out for signs.

Description: Mostly level paths. Suitable for most ages and levels of fitness and mobility, designed with flat shoes or running shoes in mind. Suitable for pushchairs.

To see: Henderson Creek, historical sites.

Time: approx. 60 minutes (about 5kms).

Cafés: The Falls Restaurant

Public toilets: Tui Glen Reserve

Children's playgrounds: Tui Glen Reserve (includes a flying fox)

Dogs: Off leash exercise areas: within reserves and parks.

Picnic Sites: Take your own rugs and picnic gear.

Directions:

Start from the corner of Edmonton Road and Alderman Drive.

1. Enter Falls Park via the entrance in front of The Falls Restaurant.
2. Cross the yellow bridge to the right > to Tui Glen Reserve.
3. Take the next left < to enter the "International Walkway of Trees".
4. Keep going straight ahead (do not turn right under the road bridge), to exit on the footpath of Central Park Drive.
5. Take the very next road to the left < and after the business sign, turn left < into Epping Esplanade (not sign posted).
6. Exit straight ahead into Epping Road and continue along Buscomb Avenue.
7. Turn left < into Millstream Drive.
8. Turn right < just before #37 Millstream Drive onto pathway leading to Falls Park.
9. Take the next path to the left < and continue around the circumference of Falls Park to continue alongside Henderson Creek to return to the start.

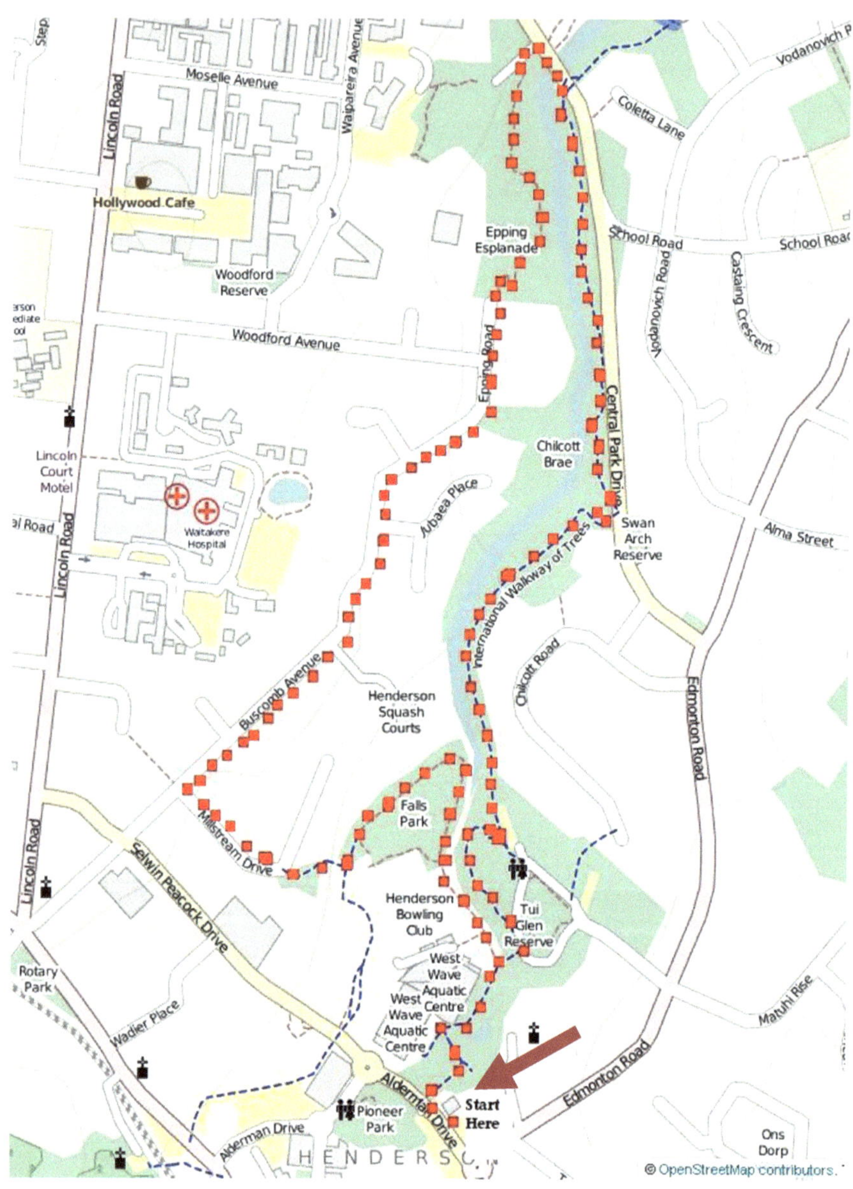

Moselle Avenue
Waiparera Avenue
Lincoln Road
Step
Vodanovich P
Coletta Lane
School Road
School Road
Hollywood Cafe
Woodford Reserve
Epping Esplanade
Castaing Crescent
Vodanovich Road
erson ediate ol
Woodford Avenue
Epping Road
Central Park Drive
Lincoln Court Motel
Chilcott Brae
Swan Arch Reserve
Alma Street
al Road
Lincoln Road
Waitakere Hospital
Jubaea Place
International Walkway of Trees
Busscomb Avenue
Henderson Squash Courts
Chilcott Road
Edmonton Road
Millstream Drive
Falls Park
Selwin Peacock Drive
Henderson Bowling Club
Tui Glen Reserve
Rotary Park
West Wave Aquatic Centre
West Wave Aquatic Centre
Matuhi Rise
Wadier Place
Alderman Drive
Start Here
Edmonton Road
Pioneer Park
Ons Dorp
Alderman Drive
H E N D E R S O
© OpenStreetMap contributors.

RESOURCES

Auckland Council – current dog regulations:

aucklandcouncil.govt.nz/EN/licencesregulations/dogsandanimals/
Pages/home.aspx

Dog friendly web sites:

doogle.co.nz
fetchmag.co.nz
planmyplay.co.nz/spotlight/auckland-special-interest-dog-
friendly-exercise-areas-beaches
localist.co.nz/auckland/articles/top-10-auckland-dog-parks

Dog friendly beaches and other areas. Please check Auckland Council website and signage for current regulations.

1. Takapuna, Cheltenham and North Head on the North Shore.
2. Kakamatua on Manukau Harbour.
3. Kauri Point on the North Shore.
4. Mission Bay and Kohimarama along Tamaki Drive.
5. Mellons Bay near Howick.
6. Taipari Strand, Taikata Road, Te Atatu Peninsula.
7. Waikowhai Park off Hillsborough Road

ABOUT THE AUTHORS

For many years, Helen and her friend Grace talked as they walked around Cornwall Park and One Tree Hill. One day, Grace turned to Helen and said "Would you like a change from walking around here?" Helen replied "Yes, but where would we go?"

And that was the beginning of the Mini Adventures for Maximum Enjoyment – for Health, Fitness and Fun. Grace scouted out the routes, the girls would get lost at times, but they walked on. And then Grace bought herself a smart phone and even though they still got lost, they could tell where they were from the map on the phone.

The walks had to comply with strict criteria – first of all, they had to be circular, each walk had to provide interest and a 'wow' factor, if there was a café nearby even better. But most of all, they had to be fun and enjoyable – not tedious.

The walks in this book have all been traversed (more than once) by Helen and Grace (and documented by Helen) so that the walker has very little chance of getting lost.

"Short Walks in Auckland website has been brilliant find for Sport Waitakere as we are both working towards a common goal."

**Emma Haigh | Active Communities Advisor |
Sport Waitakere**

On behalf of The University of Auckland, I would like to thank Helen for the custom route maps she has produced for our popular 'Walk the Talk' programme. The maps are perfect for our needs, professionally made and well received by participants.

**Hugh Markham, Active Recreation Manager,
The University of Auckland**

More walk guides available at
www.walksinauckland.co.nz

CURRENT TITLES IN THIS SERIES

Volcanoes
Coastal Walks (part one)
Coastal Walks (part two)
Urban Bush
Dog Friendly Walks (part one)
Dog Friendly Walks (part two)

Available from Amazon.com and Auckland Libraries